From a Seed to a Tree

By Maggie Vaughn

In this field is a beech tree.

Let's study it!

Its branches have pods
with spikes on them.

There are seeds inside the pods,
but we cannot see them yet.

The pods crack.

We can see two seeds
in the pod.

Some pods have three seeds!

The seeds drop down to the field.

Then the seeds “sleep”
for a while.

They need the sun
to heat them up.
So, they wait for spring.

Sweet dreams, seeds!

Rain seeps deep into the field.

The seeds drink up the rain.

In spring, a seedling peeks out.

A seedling is a baby plant.

The seedling makes green leaves.

The leaves reach up
to the sun.

The seedling is weak,
but the sun makes it strong.

A ceiling of branches shields the seedling from too much sun.

As weeks go by,
the seedling grows.

It's still a baby,
but it's a real tree!

It could be as tall as a chimney one day.

Then that beech tree will drop its seeds!

CHECKING FOR MEANING

1. When can we see the seeds inside the seed pod? *(Literal)*
2. What are some things seeds and seedlings need so they can grow? *(Literal)*
3. Why would too much sun be bad for a plant? *(Inferential)*

EXTENDING VOCABULARY

field	Which letters make the long /ē/ sound in the word *field*? Describe a field. How is it different to a park?
weak	Which letters make the long /ē/ sound in the word *weak*? What is a word that means the opposite of weak?
chimney	What sounds are in the word *chimney*? Which letters make the long /ē/ sound? What is a chimney used for?

MOVING BEYOND THE TEXT

1. Other than a chimney, what other tall objects could the author have used to describe the height of the trees?
2. Have you ever grown a plant, flower or tree? How did you take care of it? What type of plant would you like to grow?
3. What are some other plants that have seeds or grow from seeds? Think about different kinds of fruit.
4. Trees grow in lots of different places. Where have you seen trees growing?

TIME TO WRITE

Write about a tree or flower you like. Why do you like it?

PRACTICE WORDS

be
chimney
field
beech
tree
see
green
study
sleep
heat
we
seed
seeds
three
sweet
seeps
dreams
need
seedling
deep
reach
peeks
weak
baby
leaves
weeks
ceiling
real
shields